Chili

A fiery feast of red-hot recipes

Linda Doeser

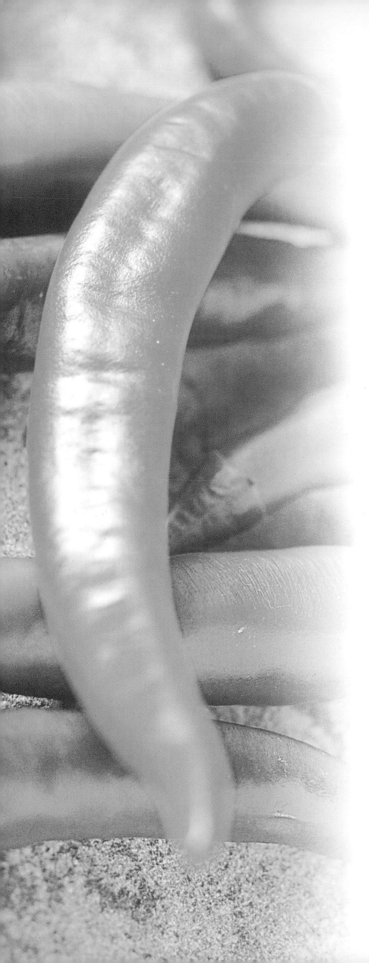

This is a Parragon Publishing Book
First published in 2004

Parragon Publishing
Queen Street House
4 Queen Street
Bath
BA1 1HE
United Kingdom

ISBN: 1-40542-952-6

Printed in Indonesia

Produced by the BRIDGEWATER BOOK COMPANY LTD

Photographer: Karen Thomas
Prop Stylist: Karen Thomas
Food Stylist: Valerie Berry

Note
This book uses imperial, metric, or US cup measurements. Follow the
same units of measurement throughout; do not mix imperial and metric. All spoon
measurements are level: teaspoons are assumed to be 5 ml,
and tablespoons are assumed to be 15 ml. Unless otherwise stated, milk is assumed to be
whole, eggs and individual vegetables such as potatoes are medium, and pepper is freshly
ground black pepper.

The times given are an approximate guide only. The preparation times may differ according
to the techniques used by different people and the cooking times may vary as a result of the
type of oven used.

Recipes using raw or very lightly cooked eggs should be avoided by infants, the elderly,
pregnant women, convalescents, and anyone suffering from an illness. Pregnant and
breastfeeding women are advised to avoid eating peanuts and peanut products.

Contents

Introduction

Originally from Mexico, *where they are still an important feature of the local cuisine, chilies have been grown throughout the tropics since the 15th century and now star in dishes from the Caribbean, Africa, India, China, and Southeast Asia, as well as many other countries. They are the hot members of the pepper family and range from relatively mild to mouth-numbingly fiery.*

As a general rule, small, pointed chilies tend to be hotter than rounder varieties and red chilies tend to be milder than green ones. Most of the heat is concentrated in the membranes surrounding the seeds, so removing the seeds before use produces a milder flavor. If you have sensitive skin, be sure to wear rubber gloves when handling chilies and always avoid touching your lips, nose, and eyes until you have washed your hands.

There are several hundred varieties of chilies, and nearly 200 are grown in Mexico alone. Among the most popular medium to hot chilies are jalapeño, serrano, Fresno, Thai, Scotch bonnet, rocotillo, poblano, and, hottest of all, habanero. Milder chilies range from the sweet-flavored Anaheim and cherry varieties to banana and chilaca chilies.

Chilies may be pickled or smoked, and jalapeño is a favorite for both of these treatments. Dried chilies such as ancho, the dried version of poblano, are an invaluable pantry standby because they can be soaked in warm water to reconstitute them or they can simply be crumbled.

Whether you enjoy the thrill of a flaming-hot mouth or you prefer the more subtle side of this colorful ingredient, cooking with chilies can lend spice to your dining table all year round.

Chilies Rellenos

SERVES 4–8

PREPARATION TIME: 20 MINUTES

COOKING TIME: 15–20 MINUTES

---

3 eggs, separated

³/₈ cup all-purpose flour

11¹/₂ oz/325 g Cheddar or other
   semihard cheese

16 fresh jalapeño chilies

corn oil, for deep-frying

These spicy Mexican mouthfuls make a great appetizer or are delicious served with predinner drinks.

1 Whisk the egg whites in a dry, greasefree bowl until stiff. Beat the egg yolks in a separate bowl, then fold in the whites. Spread out the flour in a shallow dish. Cut 8 oz/225 g of the cheese into 16 sticks and grate the remainder.

2 Make a slit in the side of each chili and scrape out the seeds. Rinse the cavities and pat dry with paper towels. Place a stick of cheese inside each chili.

3 Preheat the broiler. Heat the oil for deep-frying to 350–375°F/ 180–190°C, or until a cube of bread dropped into the oil browns in 30 seconds. Dip the chilies into the egg mixture, then into the flour. Deep-fry, turning occasionally, until golden brown all over. Drain well on paper towels.

4 Arrange the chilies in an ovenproof dish and sprinkle over the grated cheese. Place under the broiler until the cheese has melted, then serve.

Guacamole

SERVES 4

PREPARATION TIME: 15 MINUTES

COOKING TIME: NONE

2 avocados

1 fresh green chili, seeded and finely chopped

2 fresh red chilies, seeded and finely chopped

1 garlic clove, finely chopped

4 scallions, finely chopped

2 tbsp olive oil, plus extra for drizzling

juice of 1 lime

salt

fresh cilantro leaves, to garnish

tortilla chips, to serve

You can also serve this fiery dip with raw vegetable sticks or spoon it over broiled steak or chops.

1 Halve the avocados and remove the pits. Using a spoon, scoop the flesh into a bowl and mash with a fork to a soft, chunky consistency.

2 Stir the chilies, garlic, scallions, olive oil, and lime juice into the mashed avocado and season to taste with salt. If you prefer a smooth dip, place the avocado flesh, chilies, garlic, scallions, oil, and lime juice in a food processor or blender and process to a purée.

3 Spoon the guacamole into a serving bowl and drizzle a little extra olive oil over the top. Sprinkle with cilantro leaves.

4 If you are not serving the guacamole immediately, cover the bowl tightly with plastic wrap to prevent discoloration and store in the refrigerator for no longer than 2 hours. Serve with tortilla chips.

Egg Rolls with Sweet Chili Dipping Sauce

These spicy Thai favorites make a wonderful first course and unusual party food.

1 For the sauce, heat the vinegar, water, and sugar in a pan, stirring to dissolve the sugar. Bring to a boil and boil, without stirring, until syrupy. Stir in the chilies and set aside. Meanwhile, soak the noodles according to the package instructions. Drain, then cut into short lengths.

2 Heat 2 tablespoons oil in a preheated wok. Add the chilies and garlic and stir-fry for 1 minute. Add the pork and stir-fry for 2 minutes, until browned. Add the Chinese cabbage, carrot, noodles, sugar, fish and oyster sauces, and stir-fry for 3 minutes. Cool.

3 Place 2 teaspoons of filling on each wrapper and roll up, tucking in the sides. Brush the edge with egg white. Heat the oil for deep-frying to 350–375°F/ 180–190°C, or until a cube of bread browns in 30 seconds. Deep-fry the rolls for 3 minutes, until golden. Drain and serve with the sauce.

MAKES 20 ROLLS

PREPARATION TIME: 30 MINUTES, PLUS 30 MINUTES COOLING
COOKING TIME: 20–25 MINUTES

3 oz/85 g cellophane noodles

2 tbsp peanut or corn oil, plus extra for deep-frying

1–2 Thai chilies, seeded and chopped

2 garlic cloves, finely chopped

1 cup fresh ground pork

3 oz/85 g Chinese cabbage, finely shredded

1 carrot, cut into thin sticks

1 tbsp sugar

2 tbsp Thai fish sauce

2 tbsp oyster sauce

20 egg roll wrappers, thawed if frozen

1 egg white, lightly beaten

For the dipping sauce

4 tbsp rice vinegar

2 tbsp water

generous 1/4 cup superfine sugar

2 Thai chilies, seeded and finely chopped

Middle Eastern Soup with Harissa

Make this soup and the harissa the day before to guarantee maximum flavor.

1 Preheat the oven to 400°F/200°C. Prick the eggplants, place on a baking sheet, and bake for 1 hour. When cool, peel and chop.

2 Heat the oil in a pan. Add the lamb and cook until browned. Add the onion, stock, and water. Bring to a boil. Reduce the heat and let simmer for 1 hour.

3 For the harissa, process the bell peppers, coriander seeds, chilies, garlic, and caraway seeds in a food processor. With the motor running, add enough oil to make a paste. Season, then spoon into a jar. Cover with oil, seal, and let chill.

4 Remove the shanks from the stock, cut off the meat, and chop. Add the sweet potato, cinnamon, and cumin to the stock, bring to a boil, cover, and let simmer for 20 minutes. Discard the cinnamon and process the mixture in a food processor with the eggplant. Return to the pan, add the lamb, and cilantro and heat until hot. Serve with the harissa.

SERVES 6

PREPARATION TIME: 30 MINUTES, PLUS
30 MINUTES COOLING

COOKING TIME: 1¹/₂ HOURS

2 eggplants

3 tbsp olive oil

6 lamb shanks

1 small onion, chopped

1³/₄ cups chicken stock

8 cups water

14 oz/400 g sweet potato, cut into chunks

2-inch/5-cm piece cinnamon stick

1 tsp ground cumin

2 tbsp chopped fresh cilantro

For the harissa

2 red bell peppers, roasted, peeled, seeded, and chopped

¹/₂ tsp coriander seeds, dry-fried

1 oz/25 g fresh red chilies, chopped

2 garlic cloves, chopped

2 tsp caraway seeds

olive oil

salt

Corn & Smoked Chili Soup

For this delicious soup you can use fresh jalapeño chilies instead of the smoked version known as chipotle chilies if you prefer.

1 Heat the oil in a large, heavy-bottom pan. Add the onions and cook over low heat, stirring occasionally, for 5 minutes, or until softened. Stir in the corn, cover, and cook for an additional 3 minutes.

2 Add the stock, half the milk, the chilies, and garlic and season with salt. Bring to a boil, reduce the heat, then cover and let simmer for 15–20 minutes.

3 Stir in the remaining milk. Set aside about ¾ cup of the soup solids, draining off as much liquid as possible. Transfer the remaining soup to a food processor or blender and process to a coarse purée.

4 Return the soup to the pan and stir in the reserved soup solids, the chorizo, lime juice, and cilantro. Reheat to simmering point, stirring constantly. Ladle into warmed bowls and serve at once.

SERVES 6

PREPARATION TIME: 20 MINUTES

COOKING TIME: 30–35 MINUTES

1 tbsp corn oil

2 onions, chopped

1 lb 4 oz/550 g frozen corn kernels, thawed

2½ cups chicken stock

scant 2 cups milk

4 chipotle chilies, seeded and finely chopped

2 garlic cloves, finely chopped

salt

2 oz/55 g thinly sliced chorizo sausage

2 tbsp lime juice

2 tbsp chopped fresh cilantro

Chili con Carne

Forget the sloppy imitations of this Tex-Mex speciality—this is the real thing.

1 Heat half of the oil in a heavy-bottom pan. Add half the chopped onion and the garlic and cook, stirring occasionally, for 5 minutes, until softened. Remove with a slotted spoon.

2 Place the flour on a plate and season, then toss the meat in the flour to coat. Cook the meat, in batches, until browned all over, then return the meat and onion to the pan. Pour in the stock and wine and bring to a boil, stirring. Reduce the heat and let simmer for 1 hour.

3 Meanwhile, heat the remaining oil in a skillet. Add the remaining onion and the red chilies and cook, stirring occasionally, for 5 minutes. Add the beans and tomatoes with their juice and break up with a wooden spoon. Let simmer for 25 minutes, until thickened.

4 Divide the meat between individual plates, top with the bean mixture, and sprinkle with the green chili. Serve with tortilla chips.

SERVES 6

PREPARATION TIME: 20 MINUTES

COOKING TIME: 1½ HOURS

4 tbsp corn oil

2 onions, chopped

1 garlic clove, chopped

1 tbsp all-purpose flour

salt and pepper

2 lb/900 g round steak, diced

1¼ cups beef stock

1¼ cups red wine

2–3 fresh red chilies, seeded and chopped

1 lb 12 oz/800 g canned red kidney beans, drained and rinsed

14 oz/400 g canned tomatoes

1 fresh green chili, seeded and sliced, to garnish

tortilla chips, to serve

Griddled Steak with Hot Chili Salsa

SERVES 4

PREPARATION TIME: 15 MINUTES

COOKING TIME: 10–15 MINUTES

4 sirloin steaks, about 8 oz/225 g each

corn oil, for brushing

salt and pepper

For the salsa

4 fresh red habanero or Scotch bonnet chilies

4 fresh green poblano chilies

3 tomatoes, peeled, seeded, and diced

2 tbsp chopped fresh cilantro

1 tbsp red wine vinegar

2 tbsp olive oil

This is a great way to serve steak cooked on a barbecue or under the broiler, and the salsa is superb with any meat.

1 First make the salsa. Preheat the broiler. Arrange the chilies on a baking sheet and cook, turning frequently, until blackened and charred. Let cool, then rub off the skins with paper towels. Halve and seed the chilies, then chop finely.

2 Mix the red and green chilies, tomatoes, and cilantro together in a bowl. Blend the vinegar and oil together in a pitcher, season with salt, and pour over the salsa. Toss well, cover, and let chill in the refrigerator until required.

3 Season the steaks with salt and pepper. Brush a grill or griddle pan lightly with oil and heat over medium heat until hot. Cook the steaks for 2–4 minutes on each side, or until cooked to your liking. Serve at once with the salsa.

Spicy Pork Kabobs with Hot Satay Sauce

SERVES 6

PREPARATION TIME: 20 MINUTES, PLUS
3 HOURS MARINATING

COOKING TIME: 20 MINUTES

Serve these tasty skewers with a refreshing crisp salad for a perfect summer meal.

1 Mix the green chilies, onion, garlic, cinnamon, cumin, ginger, bay leaves, lime rind, and juice together in a shallow dish. Add the pork, turn to coat, then cover and let marinate in the refrigerator for 3 hours.

2 Preheat the broiler or barbecue. To make the sauce, pound the chilies, peanuts, lemon grass, garlic, shallots, and cilantro in a bowl with a pestle to make a paste. Heat the peanut oil in a skillet. Add the paste and cook over low heat until golden. Stir in the remaining sauce ingredients and bring to a boil. Cover and keep warm.

3 Drain the pork and thread it onto 12 metal or presoaked wooden skewers. Brush with oil and cook under the broiler or over hot coals, turning frequently, for 8–10 minutes, until cooked through and tender. Serve at once with the sauce.

3 fresh green chilies, seeded and chopped

1 onion, sliced

4 garlic cloves, finely chopped

2-inch/5-cm piece cinnamon stick, broken

2 tsp ground cumin

1-inch/2.5-cm piece fresh gingerroot, grated

2 bay leaves

grated rind and juice of 1 lime

2 lb/900 g pork fillet, cut into cubes

corn oil, for brushing

For the sauce

2 fresh red chilies, seeded and chopped

scant 3/8 cup unsalted dry-roasted peanuts, coarsely chopped

1 lemon grass stalk, chopped

1 garlic clove, chopped

8 shallots, chopped

1 tbsp chopped fresh cilantro

1 tbsp peanut oil

1 cup canned coconut milk

1 tsp dark soy sauce

1 tbsp Thai fish sauce

2 tsp brown sugar

Pork with Chilies & Garlic

SERVES 4

PREPARATION TIME: 15 MINUTES, PLUS
10 MINUTES MARINATING

COOKING TIME: 5–7 MINUTES

1 lb 7 oz/650 g fresh lean ground pork

1 tbsp Thai fish sauce

5 red Thai chilies

3 garlic cloves

3 tbsp peanut or corn oil

1 tbsp brown sugar

2 tbsp dark soy sauce

2 tbsp oyster sauce

1–2 tbsp chicken stock or water
(optional)

fresh Thai basil sprigs, to garnish

Thai chilies are fiery, so if you prefer a milder flavor substitute another variety of red chili.

1 Mix the pork and fish sauce together in a dish and let marinate for 10 minutes.

2 If you like, halve and seed the chilies. Pound the chilies and garlic together in a mortar with a pestle to make a paste. Heat the oil in a preheated wok or heavy-bottom skillet. Add the pork and chili paste and stir-fry over high heat for 2–3 minutes, or until the meat has browned.

3 Add the sugar, soy sauce, and oyster sauce and cook, stirring constantly, for 3–4 minutes, or until the pork is cooked. If the mixture seems too dry or about to scorch, add the stock or water. Serve at once, garnished with Thai basil.

Stir-fried Chicken with Chilies & Thai Herbs

Not only do chilies feature in this dish, they also take a starring role in the garnish—not for the faint-hearted.

1 Cut off and discard the woody top part of the lemon grass stalk, leaving about 5 inches/13 cm of the bulb end, then chop very finely. Heat the oil in a preheated wok or skillet. Add the chopped chilies, lemon grass, and garlic and stir-fry for 2–3 minutes, until lightly colored.

2 Add the chicken and stir-fry for 5 minutes, or until light golden brown. Stir in the fish sauce, soy sauce, and sugar and continue to stir-fry for an additional 4–5 minutes, or until the chicken is cooked through.

3 Stir in the cilantro and the leaves from 3 of the basil sprigs. Transfer to a warmed serving dish and garnish with the sliced chilies and remaining basil.

SERVES 4

PREPARATION TIME: 10 MINUTES

COOKING TIME: 15 MINUTES

1 lemon grass stalk

3 tbsp peanut or corn oil

4 red Thai chilies, seeded and chopped

4 garlic cloves, finely chopped

1 lb 2 oz/500 g skinless boneless chicken breasts, cut into cubes

3 tbsp Thai fish sauce

1 tbsp dark soy sauce

1 tsp sugar

1 tbsp chopped fresh cilantro

4 fresh Thai basil sprigs

3 red Thai chilies, thinly sliced, to garnish

Chicken & Chili Enchiladas

Corn tortillas are wrapped round a spicy filling and baked in a tasty sauce for a substantial meal.

1 Preheat the oven to 350°F/180°C and brush a large, ovenproof dish with oil. Place two-thirds of the chilies, the onion, garlic, cilantro, lime juice, stock, tomatoes, and sugar in a food processor and pulse to a purée. Scrape into a pan and let simmer over medium heat for 10 minutes, until thickened.

2 Mix the remaining chilies, the chicken, ½ cup of the cheese and the oregano together. Season with salt and stir in half the sauce.

3 Heat the tortillas in a dry, heavy-bottom skillet or in the microwave according to the package instructions. Divide the chicken mixture between them, spooning it along the centers, then roll up and place, seam-side down, in the dish.

4 Pour the remaining sauce over the enchiladas and sprinkle with the remaining cheese. Bake in the oven for 20 minutes and serve hot.

SERVES 4

PREPARATION TIME: 25 MINUTES

COOKING TIME: 30–35 MINUTES

corn oil, for brushing

5 fresh hot green chilies, such as jalapeño or serrano, seeded and chopped

1 Spanish onion, chopped

2 garlic cloves, chopped

2 tbsp chopped fresh cilantro

2 tbsp lime juice

½ cup chicken stock

2 beefsteak tomatoes, peeled, seeded, and chopped

pinch of sugar

12 oz/350 g cooked chicken, shredded

¾ cup queso anejo or Cheddar cheese, grated

2 tsp chopped fresh oregano

salt

8 corn or flour tortillas

Indian Chili Chicken

A mixture of fresh chilies and chili powder makes this a very fiery dish—it's also packed with flavor.

1 Make a slit along the side of each chili. Heat the oil in a large, heavy-bottom skillet. Add the chilies and cook over low heat, turning occasionally, for 4–5 minutes, or until starting to color. Remove with a slotted spoon and set aside until required.

2 Add the onions, chili powder, ginger, garlic, cumin, curry leaves, and a pinch of salt to the skillet and stir-fry for 2–3 minutes. Add the chicken and continue to stir-fry for 8–10 minutes, or until tender and cooked through.

3 Stir in the chopped cilantro and lime juice, return the chilies to the skillet, and add the tomatoes. Stir briefly, then serve at once with naan bread or freshly cooked rice.

SERVES 4

PREPARATION TIME: 10 MINUTES

COOKING TIME: 15–20 MINUTES

6–8 large fresh red chilies

4 tbsp corn oil

2 onions, chopped

1 tsp chili powder

1 tsp grated fresh gingerroot

2 garlic cloves, finely chopped

1/2 tsp cumin seeds

2 curry leaves

salt

1 lb 7 oz/650 g skinless boneless chicken breasts, cut into cubes

2 tbsp chopped fresh cilantro

1 tbsp lime juice

4 tomatoes, quartered

naan bread or freshly cooked rice, to serve

Thai Green Curry

SERVES 4

PREPARATION TIME: 25 MINUTES

COOKING TIME: 15–20 MINUTES

You can make this fragrant dish with beef, shrimp, angler fish, or as here, chicken. Store leftover curry paste in the refrigerator.

1 First make the curry paste. Seed the chilies if you like and coarsely chop. Place all the paste ingredients in a mortar and pound with a pestle. Alternatively, process in a food processor. Gradually blend in the oil.

2 Heat 2 tablespoons oil in a preheated wok or large, heavy-bottom skillet. Add 2 tablespoons of the curry paste and stir-fry briefly until all the aromas are released.

3 Add the chicken, lime leaves, and lemon grass and stir-fry for 3–4 minutes, until the meat is starting to color. Add the coconut milk and eggplants and let simmer gently for 8–10 minutes, or until tender.

4 Stir in the fish sauce and serve at once, garnished with Thai basil sprigs and lime leaves.

2 tbsp peanut or corn oil

1 lb 2 oz/500 g skinless boneless chicken breasts, cut into cubes

2 kaffir lime leaves, coarsely torn

1 lemon grass stalk, finely chopped

1 cup canned coconut milk

16 baby eggplants, halved

2 tbsp Thai fish sauce

For the green curry paste

16 fresh green chilies

2 shallots, sliced

4 kaffir lime leaves

1 lemon grass stalk, chopped

2 garlic cloves, chopped

1 tsp cumin seeds

1 tsp coriander seeds

1 tbsp grated fresh gingerroot or galangal

1 tsp grated lime rind

5 black peppercorns

1 tbsp sugar

salt

2 tbsp peanut or corn oil

To garnish

fresh Thai basil sprigs

kaffir lime leaves, thinly sliced

Indonesian Chili Shrimp

This is a great dish for informal entertaining, as it tastes special but is very quick to prepare.

1 Using a sharp knife, finely chop the ginger. Shell and devein the shrimp.

2 Heat the oil in a preheated wok or large, heavy-bottom skillet. Add the ginger, garlic, shallots, and chilies and stir-fry over medium heat for 4–5 minutes, until the shallots are starting to soften. Add the shrimp and stir-fry for an additional 3–5 minutes, or until the shrimp have changed color.

3 Add the coconut milk and stir in the ground coriander and chopped cilantro. Season to taste with salt and bring to a boil. Reduce the heat and let simmer gently for 5 minutes, or until heated through.

4 Serve the shrimp at once with freshly cooked rice.

SERVES 4

PREPARATION TIME: 10 MINUTES

COOKING TIME: 15 MINUTES

1-inch/2.5-cm piece fresh gingerroot or galangal

1 lb 2 oz/500 g large raw shrimp

2 tbsp peanut or corn oil

2 garlic cloves, finely chopped

4 shallots, finely chopped

3 fresh red chilies, seeded and thinly sliced

$^2/_3$ cup canned coconut milk

1 tsp ground coriander

1 tbsp chopped fresh cilantro

salt

freshly cooked rice, to serve

Chili Crab

SERVES 4

PREPARATION TIME: 25 MINUTES

COOKING TIME: 10 MINUTES

2 cooked crabs, about 2 lb/900 g each

4 garlic cloves, chopped

1-inch/2.5-cm piece fresh gingerroot, chopped

3 fresh red chilies, seeded and chopped

4 tbsp peanut or corn oil

4 tbsp tomato ketchup

2 tbsp dark soy sauce

1 tbsp brown sugar

²/₃ cup water

chopped scallions, to garnish

Serve this fabulous dish in a large bowl and let everybody help themselves and eat the scrumptious morsels with their fingers.

1 Prepare each crab. Break off the claws, then turn the body on its back and push it out from the shell, using your thumbs. Remove and discard the stomach and "dead man's fingers." Chop the shell in half with a cleaver, cut the body section in half, and crack the claws. Grind the garlic, ginger, and chilies in a mortar with a pestle to make a paste.

2 Heat the oil in a preheated wok or large, heavy-bottom skillet. Add all the crab pieces and stir-fry for 1 minute. Add the spice paste and stir-fry for an additional 2 minutes.

3 Add the ketchup, soy sauce, sugar, and water, stir well, then cover and let simmer for 5 minutes. Transfer to a large serving bowl, garnish with the scallions and serve at once.

Fish with a Chili Crust

SERVES 4

PREPARATION TIME: 15 MINUTES

COOKING TIME: 10 MINUTES

1 small bunch fresh cilantro or
flatleaf parsley

3–4 dried red chilies, crushed

2 tbsp sesame seeds

salt and pepper

1 egg white

4 tuna steaks, about 5–6 oz/
140–175 g each

2–3 tbsp corn oil

2 limes, halved, to garnish

*This attractive and flavor-packed dish can be made with any
firm-fleshed fish, such as cod or angler fish.*

1 Chop the cilantro or parsley leaving a few leaves whole to
garnish. Mix the crushed chilies, chopped cilantro or parsley,
and sesame seeds together in a shallow dish and season to
taste with salt and pepper. Lightly beat the egg white with
a fork in a separate shallow dish.

2 Dip the tuna steaks first in the egg white, then in the chili and
herb mixture to coat. Gently pat the crust evenly over the fish
with the palm of your hand, making sure that both sides of the
steaks are well covered.

3 Heat the oil in a large, heavy-bottom skillet. Add the steaks
and cook over medium heat for 4 minutes, then turn them over
carefully, using a spatula. Cook for an additional 4 minutes,
then transfer to warmed serving plates. Garnish with the lime
and the remaining cilantro or parsley, and serve at once.

Hot Potato Patties

This is a wonderful way to spice up potatoes and, if you cook and mash them in advance, is very quick.

1 Cook the potatoes in a large pan of lightly salted boiling water for 20–25 minutes, or until tender. Drain well and mash with a fork or potato masher. Tip into a bowl and let stand until cool enough to handle.

2 Stir the chilies, almonds, coconut, cilantro, flour, and ginger into the mashed potato, mixing well, and season to taste with salt. Shape the mixture into small balls between the palms of your hands and gently flatten into patties.

3 Heat the oil for deep-frying to 350–375°F/180–190°C, or until a cube of bread dropped in the oil browns in 30 seconds. Deep-fry the patties, in batches if necessary, for 5 minutes, or until golden. Drain on paper towels and serve at once with the chutney.

SERVES 4

PREPARATION TIME: 20 MINUTES, PLUS
30 MINUTES COOLING

COOKING TIME: 30–40 MINUTES

1 lb 2 oz/500 g potatoes, peeled and
    cut into chunks

salt

2 fresh green chilies, seeded and finely
    chopped

1 fresh red chili, seeded and finely
    chopped

1 tbsp blanched almonds, finely
    chopped

2 tbsp dry unsweetened coconut

1 tbsp chopped fresh cilantro or parsley

2 tbsp all-purpose flour

1-inch/2.5-cm piece fresh gingerroot,
    grated or very finely chopped

vegetable oil, for deep-frying

mango chutney, to serve

Tapas Potatoes with Chilies

SERVES 4–6

PREPARATION TIME: 10 MINUTES
COOKING TIME: 35–40 MINUTES

2 lb 4 oz/1 kg small new potatoes, unpeeled

salt and pepper

3 dried red chilies

4 tbsp olive oil

2 garlic cloves, finely chopped

4 scallions, chopped

7 oz/200 g canned tomatoes

1 tbsp strained tomatoes

1 tbsp sherry vinegar

1/2 tsp saffron threads, crushed

Serve these potatoes as an accompaniment to a main course, or pass a dish of them round with toothpicks for a Spanish-style appetizer. They are delicious with a glass of chilled wine.

1 Cook the potatoes in a large pan of lightly salted boiling water for 10–15 minutes, or until only just tender. Drain and let stand until cool enough to handle.

2 Meanwhile, crush the chilies in a mortar with a pestle. Heat the oil in a heavy-bottom pan. Add the garlic and scallions and cook over medium heat for 5 minutes, until softened. Stir in the crushed chilies, tomatoes with their juices, strained tomatoes, sherry vinegar, and saffron and season to taste with salt and pepper. Reduce the heat and let simmer gently, stirring occasionally, for 10 minutes.

3 Cut the potatoes in half and add to the pan, stirring well to coat. Cover and let simmer gently for an additional 10 minutes. Taste, adjust the seasoning, and serve hot or at room temperature.

Singapore Noodles

This ever-popular dish is very versatile and, if you like, you can add shrimp or strips of chicken to make it even more substantial.

1 Soak the noodles in a bowl of boiling water for 10 minutes, or according to the package instructions. Meanwhile, drain the mushrooms, discard the stalks, and slice the caps. Drain the noodles and pat dry with paper towels.

2 Heat half the oil in a preheated wok or skillet. Add the noodles and a pinch of salt and stir-fry for 2 minutes. Transfer to a dish and keep warm.

3 Heat the remaining oil in the wok. Add the shallots, garlic, and chilies and stir-fry for 2–3 minutes. Stir in the curry powder and cook, stirring, for 1 minute. Add the baby corn, snow peas, green bell pepper, and Chinese cabbage and stir-fry for 5 minutes, or until the vegetables are tender but still have some "bite."

4 Stir in the mushrooms and return the noodles to the wok. Stir-fry for 2 minutes, then add the soy sauce. Serve at once.

SERVES 4

PREPARATION TIME: 15 MINUTES, PLUS 30 MINUTES SOAKING

COOKING TIME: 12 MINUTES

8 oz/225 g rice-flour noodles

1/4 cup dried Chinese mushrooms, soaked in hot water for 30 minutes

4 tbsp peanut or corn oil

salt

4 shallots, chopped

2 garlic cloves, finely chopped

2 fresh green chilies, seeded and finely chopped

2 tsp curry powder

4 oz/115 g baby corn, halved

4 oz/115 g snow peas

1 green bell pepper, seeded and sliced

4 oz/115 g Chinese cabbage, shredded

2 tbsp soy sauce

Chili Beans

Known as frijoles in Mexico, this dish is traditionally made with black Great Northern beans, but other types of bean may also be used.

1 Drain the beans, rinse well, and place in a large, heavy-bottom pan. Cover the beans with cold water, then add the bay leaf, half the chopped onion, half the chopped garlic, and the chilies. Bring to a boil and boil rapidly for 15 minutes. Reduce the heat, cover, and let simmer for 1 hour, adding more boiling water if necessary. Add 1 tablespoon of the oil and let simmer for 30–45 minutes, until tender. Season with salt and set aside.

2 Heat the remaining oil in a skillet. Add the remaining onion and garlic and cook, stirring occasionally, for 5 minutes, until softened. Add the tomatoes and cook for an additional 5 minutes.

3 Add 3 tablespoons of the cooked beans to the skillet and mash the mixture thoroughly. Stir the mixture into the remaining beans and reheat gently. Taste and adjust the seasoning, if necessary. You can turn this dish into a hearty meal by serving with grated mozzarella cheese, baby tomatoes, scallions, and flour tortillas.

SERVES 6

PREPARATION TIME: 15 MINUTES, PLUS 3–4 HOURS SOAKING

COOKING TIME: 1–1¼ HOURS

2 cups dried black Great Northern or red kidney beans, soaked for 3–4 hours

1 bay leaf

2 onions, chopped

2 garlic cloves, finely chopped

2–3 fresh green chilies

2 tbsp corn oil

salt

3 tomatoes, peeled, seeded, and chopped

To garnish

mozzarella cheese, grated

baby tomatoes

scallions

flour tortillas

Chili Vodka

SERVES 2

PREPARATION TIME: 5 MINUTES, PLUS
1 HOUR STEEPING (OPTIONAL)

COOKING TIME: NONE

³/₄ cup chili-flavored vodka

2 pickled jalapeño chilies

ice cubes

dry vermouth, to taste

To prepare your own chili vodka, steep fresh chilies in a bottle of vodka for several days, then strain and bottle once more.

1 Pour the vodka into a small pitcher. Seed the chilies, if you like, then cut 2 large slices and set aside for decoration. Add the remaining chilies to the vodka, cover with plastic wrap, and place in the freezer for 1 hour. This makes the chili flavor more pronounced, but this step may be omitted.

2 Wrap the ice cubes in a dish towel and hit with a meat mallet or rolling pin to break them up. Place the cracked ice in a mixing glass or pitcher. Pour in the vodka, add 2 dashes of vermouth for a very dry martini, or more if you prefer, and stir well until the outside of the glass is lightly frosted.

3 Strain the cocktail into 2 cocktail glasses, garnish with the reserved slices of chili, and serve at once. Tortilla chips make a great accompaniment to this exotic cocktail.

Index